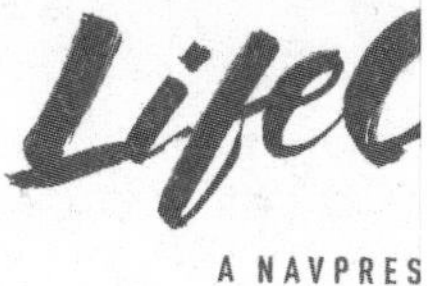

A NAVPRES

A life-changing encounter with God's Word

THE FRUIT OF THE SPIRIT

God grows His character in us as a living witness for a watching world.

A NavPress resource published in alliance with Tyndale House Publishers

NavPress is the publishing ministry of The Navigators, an international Christian organization and leader in personal spiritual development. NavPress is committed to helping people grow spiritually and enjoy lives of meaning and hope through personal and group resources that are biblically rooted, culturally relevant, and highly practical.

For more information, visit NavPress.com.

The Fruit of the Spirit: A Bible Study on Reflecting the Character of God

A NavPress resource published in alliance with Tyndale House Publishers

Written by Jack Kuhatschek

The Team:
David Zimmerman, Publisher; Caitlyn Carlson, Editor; Elizabeth Schroll, Copy Editor; Olivia Eldredge, Operations Manager; Sarah Susan Richardson, Designer

For information about special discounts for bulk purchases, please contact Tyndale House Publishers at csresponse@tyndale.com, or call 1-855-277-9400.

ISBN 978-1-64158-519-4

Printed in the United States of America

28 27 26 25 24 23 22
7 6 5 4 3 2 1

CONTENTS

HOW TO USE THIS STUDY

Objectives

The topical guides in the LifeChange series of Bible studies cover important topics from the Bible. Although the LifeChange guides vary with the topics they explore, they share some common goals:

1. to help readers grasp what key passages in the Bible say about the topic;
2. to provide readers with explanatory notes, word definitions, historical background, and cross-references so that the only other reference they need is the Bible;
3. to teach readers how to let God's Word transform them into Christ's image;
4. to provide small groups with a tool that will enhance group discussion of each passage and topic; and
5. to write each session so that advance preparation for group members is strongly encouraged but not required.

Each lesson in this study is designed to take forty-five minutes to complete.

Overview and Details

The study begins with an overview of the fruit of the Spirit. The key to interpretation for each part of this study is content (what is the referenced passage *about*?), and the key to context is purpose (what is the author's *aim* for the passage as it relates to the overall topic?). Each lesson of the study explores an element of the fruit of the Spirit, with a corresponding passage from the Bible that further illuminates that part of the fruit.

Kinds of Questions

Bible study provides different lenses and perspectives through which to engage the Scripture: observe (what does the passage *say*?), interpret (what does the passage *mean*?), and apply (how does this truth *affect* my life?). Some of the "how" and "why" questions will take some creative thinking, even prayer, to answer. Some are opinion questions without clear-cut right answers; these will lend themselves to discussions and side studies.

Don't let your study become an exercise in knowledge alone. Treat the passage as God's Word, and stay in dialogue with Him as you study. Pray, "Lord, what do You want me to see here?", "Father, why is this true?", and "Lord, how does this apply to my life?"

It is important that you write down your answers. The act of writing clarifies your thinking and helps you to remember what you're learning.

Study Aids

Throughout the guide, there are study aids that provide background information on the passage, insights from a commentary, or word studies. These aids are included in the guide to help you interpret the Bible without needing to use other, outside resources. Still, if you're interested in exploring further, the full resources are listed in the endnotes.

Scripture Versions

Unless otherwise indicated, the Bible quotations in this guide are from the New International Version of the Bible. Other versions cited are the English Standard Version and the Christian Standard Bible.

Use any translation you like for study—or preferably more than one. Ideally you would have on hand a good, modern translation such as the New International Version, the English Standard Version, the New Living Translation, or the Christian Standard Bible. A paraphrase such as *The Message* is not accurate enough for study, but it can be helpful for comparison or devotional reading.

Memorizing and Meditating

A psalmist wrote, "I have hidden your word in my heart that I might not sin against you" (Psalm 119:11). If you write down a verse or passage that challenges or encourages you and reflect on it often for a week or more, you will find it beginning to affect your motives and actions. We forget quickly what we read once; we remember what we ponder.

When you find a significant verse or passage, you might copy it onto a card to keep with you. Set aside five minutes each day just to think about what the passage might mean in your life. Recite it to yourself, exploring its meaning. Then, return to the passage as often as you can during the day for a brief review. You will soon find it coming to mind spontaneously.

For Group Study

A group of four to ten people allows the richest discussions, but you can adapt this guide for other-sized groups. It will suit a wide range of group types, such as home Bible studies, growth groups, youth groups, and workplace Bible studies. Both new and experienced Bible students, and new and mature Christians, will benefit from the guide. You can omit or leave for later any questions you find too easy or too hard.

The guide is intended to lead a group through one lesson per meeting. This guide is formatted so you will be able to discuss each of the questions at length. Be sure to make time at each discussion for members to ask about anything they didn't understand.

Each member should prepare for a meeting by writing answers for all of the background and discussion questions to be covered. Application will be very difficult, however, without private thought and prayer.

Two reasons for studying in a group are accountability and support. When each member commits in front of the rest to seek growth in an area of life, you can pray for one another, listen jointly for God's guidance, help one another resist temptation, assure each other that each person's growth matters to you, use the group to practice spiritual principles, and so on. Pray about one another's commitments and needs at most meetings. If you wish, you can spend the first few minutes of each meeting sharing any results from applications prompted by previous lessons and discuss new applications toward the end of the meeting. Follow your time of sharing with prayer for these and other needs.

If you write down what others have shared, you are more likely to remember to pray for them during the week, ask about what they shared at the next meeting, and notice answered prayers. You might want to get a notebook for prayer requests and discussion notes.

Taking notes during discussion will help you remember to follow up on ideas, stay on the subject, and have clarity on an issue. But don't let note-taking keep you from participating.

Some best practices for groups:

1. If possible, come to the group discussion prepared. The more each group member knows about the passage and the questions being asked, the better your discussion will be.
2. Realize that the group leader will not be teaching from the passage but instead will be facilitating your discussion. Therefore, it is important for each group member to participate so that everyone can contribute to what you learn as a group.
3. Try to stick to the passage covered in the session and the specific questions in the study guide.

4. Listen attentively to the other members of the group when they are sharing their thoughts about the passage. Also, realize that most of the questions are open-ended, allowing for more than one answer.

5. Be careful not to dominate the discussion—especially if you are the leader. Allow time for everyone to share their thoughts and ideas.

6. As mentioned previously, throughout the session are study aids that provide background information on the passage, insights from a commentary, or word studies. Reading these aloud during the meeting is optional and up to the discussion leader. However, each member can refer to these insights if they found them helpful in understanding the passage.

A Note on Topical Studies

LifeChange guides offer a robust and thoughtful engagement with God's Word. The book-centric guides focus on a step-by-step walk through that particular book of the Bible. The topical studies use Scripture to help you engage more deeply with God's Word and its implications for your life.

INTRODUCTION

The Fruit of the Spirit

JESUS ONCE TOLD His disciples: "Every good tree bears good fruit, but a bad tree bears bad fruit" (Matthew 7:17). That's a reality every farmer knows: a healthy tree, rooted and fed well by its source, shows its health by the good fruit it bears. But if a tree produces poor fruit—or worse, no fruit at all—something in the health of the tree or its connection to good soil and nutrition is compromised.

Jesus elaborated, "A good tree cannot bear bad fruit, and a bad tree cannot bear good fruit. Every tree that does not bear good fruit is cut down and thrown into the fire. Thus, by their fruit you will recognize them" (verses 18-20).

Of course, we know that Jesus was not simply talking about agriculture. In Galatians 5, the apostle Paul tells us very clearly the nature of both bad and good fruit. The bad fruit, which humanity has displayed since the very first sin, includes "sexual immorality, impurity, sensuality, idolatry, sorcery, enmity, strife, jealousy, fits of anger, rivalries, dissensions, divisions, envy, drunkenness, orgies, and things like these." Paul concludes this string of sins by saying, "I warn you, as I warned you before, that those who do such things will not inherit the kingdom of God" (Galatians 5:19-21, ESV).

Good fruit, on the other hand, does not come naturally to fallen human beings and can only appear through the supernatural work of the Holy Spirit, who lives within every true Christian: "The fruit of the Spirit is love, joy, peace, patience, kindness, goodness, faithfulness, gentleness, self-control" (Galatians 5:22-23, ESV). Jesus displayed these excellent qualities throughout His life on earth because they reflect the character of God Himself. And from the moment you received Jesus as your Savior and Lord, that "fruit" has gradually and increasingly begun to appear in your life.

In this LifeChange study guide, you will look at each element of the fruit of the Spirit one session at a time, in the order that Paul presents them. Each session will focus on one key passage of Scripture that fully describes the part of the fruit being considered. The end of each session contains suggestions for studying related passages.

Jesus desires every Christian to become more fruitful every day—neither withering away nor bearing thorns, but bearing life-giving fruit. This LifeChange study guide can encourage you to fulfill His desire so that the fruit you bear will increasingly look like His.

Session One

LOVE: LEARNING TO SERVE OTHERS

Luke 10:25-37

IN 1967 BRIAN EPSTEIN walked into the Beatles' studio and announced: "Boys, I have the most fantastic news to report. You have been selected to represent England in a television program which, for the first time ever, will be transmitted live around the world via satellite."[1] John Lennon wrote the song they decided to perform—"All You Need Is Love"—two weeks before the event. During the live broadcast, the Beatles told over 350 million viewers that they could "learn how to play the game [of love]. It's easy!"

Love as part of the fruit of the Spirit, though, is a far higher calling than the "game" the Beatles suggested. And the "expert in the law" in Luke 10 probably wouldn't agree that loving God and loving others is easy—especially after Jesus tells him the parable of the Good Samaritan!

1. Read Luke 10:25-37. What are your initial impressions of how this conversation unfolds?

What do you notice about the ways Jesus responds?

2. What key words or phrases jump out at you in this passage? Why?

The expert in the law would have been familiar with Daniel 12:2: "Multitudes who sleep in the dust of the earth will awake: some to everlasting life, others to shame and everlasting contempt." Likewise, Psalm 37:18 states: "The blameless spend their days under the LORD's care, and their inheritance will endure forever."

3. The "expert in the law" decides to test Jesus' knowledge of Scripture by asking, "What must I do to inherit eternal life?" (verse 25). Why do you think he asked this specific question?

4. Jesus decides to test the one testing Him (see verse 26), and the expert answers by quoting Deuteronomy 6:5. Why is this the "greatest commandment" (Matthew 22:38)?

5. Why must our love for God be multifaceted, involving our heart, soul, strength, and mind (see verse 27)?

Darrell Bock writes: "The scribe replies with a part of the *Shema* from Deuteronomy 6:5, that portion of the Law that a Jew recited daily and that calls on the nation to love God fully. He also cites the portion of Leviticus 19:18 that calls for the love of one's neighbor. This combination was known as the 'great commandment.'"[2]

These two commands also summarize the Ten Commandments. The first four focus on our love for God, and the next six relate to loving our neighbor (Exodus 20:1-17).

6. The expert in the law also quotes Leviticus 19:18: "Love your neighbor as yourself." Why do you think the standard for loving others is the way we love ourselves (see also John 13:34)?

7. In a parallel passage, Jesus tells us, "All the Law and the Prophets depend on these two commands" (Matthew 22:40, CSB). How does it simplify your life to know that your primary goal is to love God and others?

8. After Jesus says, "Do this and you will live" (verse 28), the expert in the law tries to justify himself by asking, "And who is my neighbor?" (verse 29). How could the answer to this question make his goal of eternal life easier or more difficult?

Jesus' statement "Do this and you will live" is perplexing because it seems to imply that a person can inherit eternal life by fulfilling the law rather than by grace through faith. However, we know from Scripture that since the Fall, no one except Jesus has fulfilled the two greatest commands. Because we have all broken these commands, we need the salvation that only Jesus can provide.

9. Why do you think both the priest and the Levite refused to help the man and "passed by on the other side" (verses 31-32)?

R. T. France writes: "A Jewish audience, having heard Jesus poke fun at the religious professionals, would expect the next character to be a Jewish layman or local rabbi, whose more humane response would put the priest and the Levite to shame. That might have provoked an irreverent chuckle. The introduction instead of a Samaritan, far outside his own territory, was as deliberately shocking as if a Southern preacher before the Civil War had set up a black hero to shame the pillars of white society."[3]

10. In what specific ways did the Samaritan show love to the injured man (see verses 34-35)?

11. The expert in the law had asked, "Who is my neighbor?" How does Jesus' question in verse 36 change the nature of the question?

Why is that significant (see verses 36-37)?

12. How does God's description of love differ from how we might understand love?

How does this affect our understanding of what love will look like in our lives as we bear the fruit of the Holy Spirit?

Your Response

What would it look like for you to be a more loving neighbor at church, at work, and in your neighborhood?

For Further Study

Matthew 22:34-40 and Mark 12:28-31 are parallel passages to Luke 10:25-37. How does each one expand your understanding of the two great love commands? John 13:1-17 also provides an excellent example of how true love requires sacrificial service to others.

Session Two

JOY: REJOICING IN ANY SITUATION

Philippians 1:12-26

A FAMOUS PHOTOGRAPH by Alfred Eisenstaedt shows a sailor kissing a nurse in New York City's Times Square on August 14, 1945. All around the couple, people are smiling and laughing. What caused the sailor, later identified as George Mendonsa, to kiss a total stranger? The electronic tickers in Times Square had just announced the end of the war in the Pacific, and everyone was celebrating!

We all know that intangible, overflowing feeling of joy. Joy cannot be manufactured. Throughout Scripture, joy is not a mere emotion but something that comes directly from the work of God:

> The LORD made the heavens. Splendor and majesty are before him; strength and joy are in his dwelling place. (1 Chronicles 16:26-27)

> If you keep my commands, you will remain in my love, just as I have kept my Father's commands and remain in his love. I have told you this so that my joy may be in you and that your joy may be complete. (John 15:10-11)

> You will fill me with joy in your presence. (Psalm 16:11)

> May the God of hope fill you with all joy. (Romans 15:13)

While many events in life make us feel what we'd call joyful—our first job, our wedding day, the birth of a baby—we see in God's Word that joy is part of the deep work of the Spirit. In Philippians 1:12-26, Paul helps us understand how God equips us to choose joy in any situation.

The word for rejoice in these verses is *chairō*, which Strong's Concordance defines as "to be 'cheer'ful . . . calmly happy or well-off."[1] This word occurs seventy-four times in sixty-eight verses in the New Testament.

1. Read Philippians 1:12-26. What are the reasons Paul says he will rejoice?

2. What circumstances and situations do you see in this passage that might serve as a hindrance to joy?

3. As Paul writes this letter to the Philippians, he is in prison (either in Rome or Ephesus). How has Paul's imprisonment "actually served to advance the gospel" (Philippians 1:12)?

4. Paul's imprisonment for Christ might have made others fearful that they would share his fate if they preached the gospel. Why do you think that, instead, they became more confident and fearless (see verse 14)?

The "palace guard" (verse 13), also known as the Praetorian Guard, was "the elite bodyguard maintained at Rome by the emperors. . . . Domitian maintained ten cohorts, or approximately ten thousand men, which then became the standard. Each cohort was led by a tribune and divided into six centuries, each led by a centurion."[2]

5. What contrasting motives for preaching the gospel are mentioned in verses 15-17?

The troublemakers "imagine that as they freely seek to persuade people to join their party, Paul himself looks on with envy from his imprisonment (v. 17). Why any group would do this is impossible to determine from the distance of twenty centuries, but we know from early witnesses that Paul had a wide variety of detractors."[3]

6. Why might some Christians preach Christ "out of selfish ambition" or want to "stir up trouble" for Paul while he is in prison (verse 17)?

7. Even though Paul is in prison and in chains, which would make most people miserable, he is full of joy (see verse 18). What does this tell us about his most important values and goals in life?

8. When you face hardships or difficulties, how can your faith in Christ enable you to experience Paul's kind of joy?

People often contrast joy with happiness, claiming that the latter is dependent on our circumstances while joy transcends circumstances. Yet in Philippians 1:14 Paul is joyful because his *circumstances* have resulted in the spread of the gospel. He can rejoice because he cares more about people coming to Christ than he does about his own comfort and safety.

Frank Thielman offers this insight: "The word *soteria* ['deliverance' or 'salvation'] is commonly used in the New Testament, and especially in Paul's letters, to mean 'salvation' in the ultimate sense of rescue from God's wrath on the final day. This is clearly its meaning only a few sentences later in 1:28, where Paul contrasts the Philippians' future salvation with the destruction that awaits their persecutors. It is probably also the meaning Paul intends here, since he equates the 'deliverance' of verse 20 with Christ's being exalted in his body and says that this exaltation can happen either 'by life or by death.'"[4]

9. Paul also rejoices because he believes that the Philippians' prayers and God's provision (see verse 19) will result in his "deliverance" (NIV) or "salvation" (CSB). In light of verses 20-26, do you think Paul expects to be released from prison or to enter the presence of Christ? Why?

10. Paul states that "to me, to live is Christ and to die is gain" (verse 21). How can that outlook provide a far deeper joy than a life of self-centeredness can offer?

11. When most people face a life-threatening situation, they normally think it would be "better by far" (verse 23) if they lived rather than died. Why do you think Paul feels the opposite?

12. The Holy Spirit produces unshakeable joy in our lives, regardless of circumstance. What are ways you can seek a deeper connection with the Spirit's work and promptings so that His joy might be manifested in you?

Your Response

Throughout this passage, Paul finds joy in sacrificial service to Christ and his fellow believers. To what extent does that mirror your own outlook on life?

What can you do to more fully follow Paul's example?

For Further Study

In John 15:11, Jesus tells His disciples: "I have told you this so that my joy may be in you and that your joy may be complete." What does Jesus tell them in verses 1-17 that would give them joy?

Session Three

PEACE: OVERCOMING ANXIETY

Philippians 4:4-9

MANY PEOPLE ARE anxious about their jobs, their health, or their finances. Although Christians are certainly not immune to such feelings, the Scriptures tell us how we can find peace in the Lord even in the midst of anxious circumstances.

Many of us think of peace as an *absence* of something—conflict, stress, anxiety, fear. But the peace offered to us through the Holy Spirit is more than simply not experiencing what might disrupt our lives. As Paul writes to the Philippians, he is in prison awaiting trial and possible execution. No one would blame him for feeling anxious and fearful. Yet he is full of peace. How is that possible? In this passage, Paul urges the Philippians to adopt his attitude in the face of stressful circumstances.

1. Read Philippians 4:4-9. What key words or phrases do you notice?

What is the tone of the passage?

2. What elements do you notice that may be connected to possessing "the peace of God"?

Paul tells the Philippians not to be "frightened in any way by those who oppose you" (Philippians 1:28). In contrast to being frightened, Paul tells them how they can find peace (4:6-9). Paul also knows that some in the church might be tempted to retaliate against those who are persecuting them. In contrast to retaliation, he tells them to be gentle (4:5).

3. Paul urges his readers: "Let your gentleness be evident to all" (verse 5). The word translated as *gentleness* (NIV) implies showing kindness even in the face of unkindness. How can a gentle response enable us to live at peace with other Christians and those who don't know Christ?

4. According to verse 6, what is Paul's antidote to worry and anxiety, regardless of the situation we face?

5. Why is it important to balance our prayer requests with thanksgiving?

In his commentary on Philippians, Frank Thielman writes: "The words 'be anxious' (*merimnao*, 4:6) can refer to being unduly concerned about anything, but it is often used in contexts where persecution is the issue." He goes on to say that "the term 'guard' (*phroureo* [v. 7]) likewise is a figure drawn from the arena of conflict and is frequently used to refer to the action of a military garrison stationed inside a city."[1]

6. It doesn't make sense to feel peaceful when facing something that normally makes us anxious. How does Paul assure us that God can calm our fears—even when we can't figure out how this works (see verse 7)?

7. How can focusing on what is true, noble, right, pure, lovely, admirable, excellent, and praiseworthy help us to overcome our anxiety and feel at peace (see verse 8)?

8. Why is it crucial for us to put into practice what we have learned from Paul and the rest of Scripture (see verse 9)?

9. In verse 7 Paul promised that the Philippians would experience the "peace of God" in response to their prayers and thanksgiving. In verse 9 he promises that the "God of peace" will be with them as they follow Paul's example. How are these two promises interconnected?

10. In the Old Testament, the word often used for *peace* was שָׁלוֹם (*shalom*). This word indicates a wholeness or completeness versus an absence of anxiety or fear.[2] How might *shalom* help us better understand the Holy Spirit's work in filling us with His peace?

Your Response

If you are feeling worried or anxious about a situation you're facing, spend time in prayer and thanksgiving now, knowing that the God of peace will be with you and will also grant you peace in your heart and mind.

For Further Study

Read Matthew 6:25-34, where Jesus explains the futility of worry. How does this passage add to what you have learned in Philippians 4:4-9?

Look, too, at Psalm 46. What contrasts do you see between life within the city of God and the state of the world outside (see also John 16:33)?

Session Four

PATIENCE: THE BENEFITS OF WAITING

James 5:7-11

DOES IT BOTHER you when your checkout line is slower than the one next to you? When a slow car pulls in front of you, do you immediately change lanes? When you arrive at your doctor's office on time, how do you feel after sitting in the waiting room for half an hour? Have you ever been reluctant to pray for patience, fearing what the Lord might bring into your life to teach you patience?

Being patient is a universal human struggle. But the Holy Spirit equips us with an extraordinary kind of patience, far beyond what you need to overcome minor inconveniences. Through the power of the Spirit, we can, in the words of biblical scholar Joseph Henry Thayer, "be of a long spirit, not . . . lose heart."[1] This patience is *endurance* in the face of hard things. In James 5:7-11, the author focuses on one of the most difficult situations where we need the Spirit to bear the fruit of patience in us: when we experience suffering.

Note: It is important to view this passage in context. In the six verses that precede this passage, James condemns unjust landowners who have failed to pay their workers, closed their ears to the cries of their harvesters, fattened themselves while others are slaughtered, and condemned and murdered the innocent. This is the type of suffering that James's readers have been experiencing—in addition to being persecuted for their faith.[2]

1. Read James 5:7-11. What specific elements of patience do you glean from this passage?

Confidence in the Lord's ultimate work and authority should influence how we navigate relational struggles. According to Thayer's Greek Lexicon, the word used in this passage indicates "to be patient in bearing the offences and injuries of others; to be mild and slow in avenging; to be . . . slow to anger, slow to punish."[3]

2. What perspective equips us to be patient?

3. James tells his readers to "be patient . . . until the Lord's coming" (verse 7). How does this speak to both the duration and the ultimate remedy of Christian suffering?

4. James offers three examples of patience in this passage: farmers, the prophets, and Job. What can we learn from farmers about patience (see verse 7)?

5. How does the farmer's example apply to the Lord's coming (see verse 8)?

New Testament scholar Dan McCartney states: "Although grumbling may seem to be a minor offense, James's warning against it is serious. To say the judge is 'at the doors' surely is to indicate that the day of judgment is imminent." Further, the "overall Christian context suggests that the judge is Jesus."[4]

6. Why might impatience cause us to "grumble against one another" (verse 9)?

7. How can our realization that the day of judgment is imminent ("the Judge is standing at the door") provide the antidote to our grumbling?

8. James's second example is the prophets (see verse 10). The author of Hebrews includes the prophets when he says: "They went about in sheepskins and goatskins, destitute, persecuted and mistreated. . . . These were all commended for their faith, yet none of them received what had been promised" (Hebrews 11:37, 39). What does the prophets' example show us about living out godly patience?

9. What does James mean when he says, "As you know, we count as blessed those who have persevered" (verse 11)?

"James refers to these OT examples of faith to show not how extraordinary people of extraordinary power did marvels, but how ordinary people who shared the common human experience of suffering became extraordinary through their persevering faith in the face of adversity."[5]

How were the prophets blessed?

10. James's final example of patience and perseverance is Job (see verse 11). Based on what you know about the book of Job, why is he a good example for us today?

11. How does patience help us exhibit the other aspects of the fruit of the Spirit (love, joy, peace, kindness, goodness, faithfulness, gentleness, self-control)?

Your Response

How do hardships, difficulties, or painful experiences make you impatient?

What have you learned from the examples in this passage that can equip you to pursue patience in the midst of suffering?

For Further Study

Read and reflect on Hebrews 11. How do these people of faith demonstrate patience, perseverance, and hope?

Session Five

KINDNESS: CARING FOR ONE ANOTHER

Ruth 2

DURING THE SUMMER OF 1936, a Black athlete named Jesse Owens went to Berlin to represent the United States in the Olympics. Owens's decision was a brave one, a choice to face down explicit prejudice: Adolf Hitler's hope in hosting the Olympic games in Berlin was to prove Aryan superiority to the world.

During qualifiers for the long-jump event, Owens's foot twice crossed the foul line, putting in danger his chances of competing. At that point, his strongest rival, a German competitor named Luz Long, told Owens that he could easily qualify if he jumped just before reaching the marker. Owens later wrote about Long's act of kindness: "What I remember most was the friendship I struck up with Luz Long. He was my strongest rival, yet it was he who advised me to adjust my run-up in the qualifying round and thereby helped me to win."[1] After Owens made the jump, Luz continued to choose kindness, congratulating his rival. "Hitler must have gone crazy watching us embrace," Owens said.[2] In the midst of tremendous pressure and tensions with global ramifications, Luz Long chose active kindness—moving toward another person to care for him, no matter the cost.

Biblical kindness isn't benign goodwill. There's a cost, a choice to do good, emerging from the prompting, conviction, and power of the Holy Spirit. The story of Ruth shows us how God uses kindness for His purposes and glory.

---

1. Read Ruth 2. Whom do we see Ruth interact with in this passage?

What do you observe from their interactions with her (or lack thereof)?

2. What key moments in this passage jump out at you?

3. We know from the previous chapter in Ruth that Naomi had lost her husband and two sons while living in Moab and that she was considered "too old" to remarry (Ruth 1:12). How had those losses made both Naomi and Ruth vulnerable?

Old Testament professor Lawson Younger states the following about Naomi's situation in Moab: She has "no husband, no sons, no land, no food, no hope, no future—and she is a foreigner!"[3]

4. How did God provide, in part, for poor people like Ruth and Naomi (see Leviticus 23:22; Ruth 2:2-3)?

Younger explains: "Although the Law (Lev 19:9-10; 23:22; Deut 24:19-21) provided a legal right to glean specifically to the poor, the resident alien, the widow, and the orphan, it is clear from other passages that these people were not always granted permission to glean. Hence, the simplest understanding of Ruth's words in the last clause of verse 2 'behind anyone in whose eyes I find favor' is that 'she wants to glean behind someone who would benevolently allow it.'"[4]

5. How might Leviticus 23:22 guide us in stewarding the money and resources the Lord has given us?

Boaz is described in verse 1 as "a man of standing," which "designates one who possesses social standing and a good reputation. In this context, it connotes not only wealth and status but also ability, honor, and capability. Thus it is clearly used as a description of character."[5]

6. After Boaz learns about Ruth from his overseer (see verses 5-7), how does he go above and beyond Old Testament law in showing kindness to Ruth (see verses 8-9)?

7. Ruth is astonished by the kindness of Boaz—especially since she is a foreigner (see verse 10). What do we learn about Ruth's own kindness and character through Boaz's response to her (see verses 11-12)?

"Boaz wishes that Yahweh will 'repay' (*shlm*) Ruth for her actions and prays that she may 'be richly rewarded by the LORD, the God of Israel, under whose wings you have come to take refuge' (v. 12). Boaz specifies that Yahweh is the God 'under whose wings' (*kenapim*) Ruth has sought refuge/asylum. The word *kanap* . . . connotes the image of a bird tenderly protecting its young. Like a defenseless starling, Ruth sits securely under Yahweh's mighty wings."[6]

8. Our kindness should never emerge from a selfish motive or come with an expectation of receiving something in return. Yet kindness to others often becomes unintentionally reciprocal. Why might this be?

Lawson Younger states the following: "When Ruth resumes gleaning, Boaz orders his workers to let her glean between the sheaves themselves without trouble and even commands them without fail to pull out stalks of grain from the handfuls the men cut and leave them behind for her—an unheard-of favor. He concludes by charging them once again not to drive her away."[7]

9. In verses 14-17, what exceptional privileges does Boaz grant to Ruth, both directly and indirectly?

10. Ruth returns to Naomi with both a meal and about thirty pounds (see verse 17 footnote) of barley—an extraordinary amount. How does this entire passage, including Ruth and Naomi's conversation, reveal God's kindness and care for the two women?

11. The kindness of Boaz had implications far beyond his and Ruth's lives: because of his decision to act with goodness toward someone in need, Boaz and Ruth eventually married, becoming ancestors of both King David and Jesus. When the Holy Spirit prompts us toward kindness, God is up to something, even if we never see the end result. When have you experienced God's conviction to show kindness to another person?

What happened, and what did you learn about listening to the Holy Spirit's voice?

Your Response

Who among your family, friends, and neighbors needs help and kindness? What specific acts of kindness might you offer to them, this week and beyond?

For Further Study

The book of Ruth is a fascinating story that unfolds over only four chapters. Take time to read the rest of the book this week. What more do you learn about kindness—both human and divine?

Session Six

GOODNESS: OVERCOMING EVIL WITH GOOD

Romans 12:17-21

ON JUNE 25, 2010, on the streets of a North African city, gunshots rang out in the early morning air. An American missionary lay dead on the ground, killed by terrorists angry about the work he and his family had been doing in their country. Hours later, two high-level government officials from the Muslim republic sat in a living room with the man's wife, Emily. They had tears in their eyes, an unheard-of expression of public emotion for Muslim men. "Your husband was a good man," one of them said.[1]

The missionary's family could have walked away in the face of such a horrific tragedy. They could have left the country forever and never looked back. Instead, they have continued the work in that North African nation, continuing to choose goodness among people God loves.

When we are faced with evil, our natural reaction is to retaliate. Alfred Hitchcock once said, "Revenge is sweet and not fattening." But the Holy Spirit equips us to live differently, to choose the good. One definition of the word used for *goodness* in Galatians 5 is "uprightness of heart and life."[2] When we pursue goodness, we live rightly in relation to other human beings, choosing to be upright in every aspect of our inner and outer worlds. In Romans 12, Paul teaches us how to do this when we are faced with evil and most tempted to turn from "uprightness of heart and life."

1. Read Romans 12:17-21. What words and phrases seem most significant to you?

2. What does this passage indicate about the choice toward goodness?

3. Paul tells his readers, "Do not repay anyone evil for evil" (verse 17). Here and in verse 14, how does he echo Jesus' teaching (see Matthew 5:44; Luke 6:27-28)?

4. In contrast to retaliation, why is it important for Christians to "do what is right in the eyes of everyone" (verse 17)?

5. In a fallen and sinful world, Paul's command to "live at peace with everyone" (verse 18) seems impossible. How does he make this command more realistic by adding, "If it is possible" and "as far as it depends on you"?

New Testament scholar Douglas Moo writes: "Christians are to do what they can to find approval with non-Christians and to live at peace with them (v. 18c). But they must never seek approval with the world at the expense of God's moral demands; this means that harmonious relationships with unbelievers will not always lie in our power to achieve."[3]

6. What kinds of thoughts or actions would help you become more of a peacemaker?

7. Paul commands us, "Do not take revenge" (verse 19), assuring us that God will deal with our enemies. How does releasing our need to retaliate help us orient our motivations toward goodness?

"Believers are not to seek revenge," Moo writes. "One reason why they should not do so is that God himself is the one who avenges wrong. 'It is mine to avenge; I will repay,' says God in Deuteronomy 32:35. God knows all things, sees all things, and has all power. He is a perfectly just God, who will not ultimately allow evil to go unpunished."[4]

8. In verse 20 Paul quotes from Proverbs 25:21-22. Why is it so difficult to treat our enemies this way?

9. Most commentators believe that the phrase "heap burning coals on his head" refers to our enemies becoming ashamed of their actions.[5] Why might a posture of goodness toward those who wish us harm cause this response?

10. Paul tells his readers, "Do not be overcome by evil, but overcome evil with good" (verse 21). How might a Christian be "overcome by evil"?

How does allowing the Holy Spirit to produce goodness as our first response "overcome evil"?

Your Response

Can you identify a person or situation in your life where exercising goodness might overcome evil?

For Further Study

Read 1 Corinthians 4:9-13. How have Paul and his coworkers suffered because they serve Jesus Christ?

How do they respond to those who treat them badly?

How can you follow their example?

Session Seven

FAITHFULNESS: KEEPING OUR COMMITMENTS

Matthew 25:14-30

WHEN THE FAMOUS Italian violinist Niccolò Paganini died in 1840, his remarkable violin was given to the city of Genoa. The violin was made by the Italian luthier Bartolomeo Giuseppe Guarneri and is now considered a national treasure. It is normally kept in a museum in a clear, secure case so that people can see it even if they cannot hear it. The violin, created to make beautiful music, is rarely played in public.

In the parable of the talents ("bags of gold" in the NIV), Jesus reflects on the lives of three men who were each given a sum of money to invest by their master. One of the men chose to bury his talent in the ground instead of investing it as his master intended. The parable demonstrates the importance of being faithful to God by using the gifts He has given us.

Paul uses the Greek noun *pistis* ("faith" or "faithfulness") in the fruit of the Spirit passage of Galatians 5. Here in the parable of the talents, the related adjective *pistos* ("faithful") is used in the positive description of the first two servants. The faithfulness emerging from the work of the Holy Spirit in our lives is a conviction, a deep belief in God (*pistis*). That deep belief in the one we follow compels us to be trustworthy and reliable (*pistos*) in what He's called us to do.[1]

1. Read Matthew 25:14-30. What do you observe about the master in this account?

2. In this passage, Jesus states that the kingdom of heaven "will be like a man going on a journey, who called his servants and entrusted his wealth to them" (verse 14). What observations can you make about the kingdom of heaven based on Jesus' words in this parable?

3. Jesus uses this parable to demonstrate to His disciples how they should await His return and the fulfillment of the kingdom of heaven. What do the similarities and differences between the three servants (see verses 14-18) show us about waiting well for Christ's return?

4. What gifts, abilities, and opportunities has the Lord entrusted to you?

New Testament scholar D. A. Carson writes: "Modern English uses the word 'talent' ['bag of gold' in the NIV] for skills and mental powers God has entrusted to men; but in NT times the 'talent' (GK *5419*) was a unit of exchange. . . . It is more sensible to compare the talent with modern currency in terms of earning power. If a talent was worth 6,000 denarii, then it would take a day laborer twenty years to earn so much. So the sums are vast."[2]

"The accounting begins 'after a long time,' the implication being that the consummation of the kingdom will be long delayed (24:48; 25:5). 'Settled accounts' is a standard commercial term. The first servant, who doubled his five talents, is praised especially for his faithfulness and is given two things: increased responsibility and a share in his master's 'joy.' Jesus suggests by this that the consummated kingdom will provide glorious new responsibilities and holy delight (cf. Ro 8:17)."[3]

5. How do the first two servants demonstrate their faithfulness to the master, and how does he reward them (see verses 19-23)?

6. Why is our faithfulness to the Lord more important than the amount He has entrusted to us?

7. How does the third man view his master (see verses 24-25)?

How does this inform his justification of his actions?

8. What types of excuses might people make today for failing to use their God-given gifts in the service of Jesus Christ?

New Testament Professor Michael J. Wilkins comments: "The way he conceives of him ('you are a hard man, harvesting where you have not sown and gathering where you have not scattered seed') causes him to fear and then to hide away the talent and not seek to advance the master's capital. The servant's misperception of the master has produced alienation, mistrust, fear, and then personal sloth. Had he truly loved his master, he would not have attempted to place the blame on him but would have operated out of love."[4]

9. How does the master use the wicked servant's own words to prove his unfaithfulness (see verses 26-27)?

10. In the context of this passage, how would you explain the principle that "whoever has will be given more, and they will have an abundance. Whoever does not have, even what they have will be taken from them" (verse 29; see also verse 28)?

"The punishment is not simply taking away the talent from the wicked slave, now called 'worthless.' The master instructs that he should be thrown 'outside, into the darkness, where there will be weeping and gnashing of teeth.' As in the other parables, the contrast is between those whose eternal destiny is salvation in the presence of the long-expected Son of Man and eternal damnation. The first two servants are true disciples; the third is not. A person's faithfulness is evidence as to whether he or she is truly one of Jesus' own."[5]

11. How does faithfulness (*pistis*)—your conviction in who God is, your deep belief in Him—compel you to be faithful (*pistos*) in what He's called you to do?

Your Response

As you have been faithful with what God has entrusted to you, have you seen Him entrust you with more? If so, how?

How might He be asking you to be more faithful in what He's given you to do?

For Further Study

Read the parable of the ten minas in Luke 19:11-27. What additional insights do you gain about being a faithful steward from this version of the parable?

Session Eight

GENTLENESS: A PARENT'S CARE

1 Thessalonians 2:7-12

As I WRITE THIS, our son and daughter-in-law are visiting us with their fifteen-month-old son. They are thrilled to be parents, and Trevor is their pride and joy. This week we have watched them play with him, read books to him, feed and change him, and smother him with kisses. Their gentle and loving care for him is beautiful to behold.

As with other aspects of the fruit of the Spirit, gentleness is active, a choice to engage with another human with concern and care for their well-being. Author Matt Mikalatos notes:

> Cultivating gentleness requires a greater awareness of people around me and a more honest awareness of myself. . . . Gentleness requires us to stop and be aware of our own strength and the complicated vulnerabilities of the world around us. You are stronger than you think, and the world is more fragile than you might suspect.[1]

In 1 Thessalonians 2, Paul uses the imagery of a nursing mother and a caring father to describe his relationship to the Thessalonians. Although the word *gentleness* isn't used in the NIV, it is the preferred translation in the ESV and CSB ("We were gentle among you, like a nursing mother taking care of her own children"; verse 7, ESV). Either way, Paul demonstrates gentleness in every verse.

1. Read 1 Thessalonians 2:7-12. What words does Paul use to describe those in the church at Thessalonica?

2. How would you describe Paul's tone and posture toward his readers?

The Greek word for gentleness in Galatians 5:23 is *prautēs*, meaning "gentleness of spirit, meekness."[2] The adjective form of this word is *praus*, and we see Jesus describe Himself with this word in Matthew 11:29: "Take my yoke upon you and learn from me, for I am gentle and humble in heart, and you will find rest for your souls."

3. Paul assumes his readers will know how a "nursing mother cares for her children" (verse 7). What does this example indicate about gentleness as both action and internal posture?

4. Why do you think Paul chose that specific imagery to describe his relationship with the Thessalonians?

Michael Holmes writes: "There is a much-debated textual variant in 2:7. While a small number of manuscripts read 'gentle' (*epioi*), a substantial majority read 'infants' (*nepioi*). The single-letter difference between the two readings, however, is so slight in Greek (which was written in all capitals with no spaces between words) . . . that either reading could be explained as a scribal slip for the other one. . . . [The context] clearly favors 'gentle' . . . over 'infants.'"[3]

5. Although Paul's primary goal was to preach the gospel, how did he and his companions go far beyond that? Why (see verses 8-9)?

"The Thessalonians had become 'so dear' (i.e., *agapetoi*, 'beloved') both to God (cf. 1:4) and to Paul, Silas, and Timothy," Holmes explains. "The apparent parallelism between 2:7-9 (as a nurse fulfills her duty by caring for others and goes beyond duty in cherishing her own, so the missionaries fulfill their obligations by sharing the gospel and go beyond obligation by sharing themselves) suggests that the development of such deep affection was perhaps unexpected, though certainly welcome. That is, it is not clear that the formation of such *deep* personal friendships was part of the missionaries' original strategy. If so, then we get a glimpse here of how preaching the gospel transformed not only the hearers but also the preachers."[4]

6. Why is sharing our lives with others a vital part of sharing the gospel?

7. Many preachers have disgraced themselves and disillusioned their followers by living a double life. In contrast, what characterized Paul's life? (Look at each key word in verse 10.)

8. Why is it so important for our lives to reflect our message and our beliefs?

"Because his behavior was proper in the sight of both God and humans, Paul can say he acted 'blamelessly' (*amemptos*)," Holmes writes. "That is, no charge can be brought against him when he is examined by God (2:4)."[5]

9. Why do you think Paul switches his metaphor from a nursing mother to a caring father (see verses 11-12)?

What new dimension does that add?

Michael Holmes comments: "Paul's view of the 'kingdom' follows closely the teachings of Jesus. The kingdom indicates God's righteous 'rule' or 'dominion,' a dynamic rather than a static concept (in contrast to 'realm'). The kingdom has already been inaugurated in the ministry of Jesus, and thus is to some extent present and experienced now (Rom. 14:17; 1 Cor. 4:20), but its full manifestation and experience lies in the future, when God will vindicate his people and fully establish his rule over all creation (2 Thess. 1:5). . . .

Paul links 'glory' closely with 'kingdom' (they share a single preposition and article, and a single 'his' governs both words). The two terms together indicate a believer's ultimate goal: to live under the dominion and in the presence of God."[6]

10. How should the anticipation of God's "kingdom and glory" motivate you to "live lives worthy of God" (verse 12)?

11. What might be the impact of gentleness on our relationships with those who don't know God?

How does bearing the fruit of gentleness in our lives make way for the good news of Jesus to go forth?

Your Response

How do Paul's examples of a nurturing mother and a caring father demonstrate how we are to treat each other in the body of Christ?

In what practical ways can you follow Paul's example this week?

For Further Study

What do you learn about gentleness from each of the following passages?

Proverbs 15:1; 25:15

Matthew 11:29

Philippians 4:5

Colossians 3:12

1 Peter 3:15

Session Nine

SELF-CONTROL: MASTERING OUR DESIRES

1 Corinthians 9:24–10:13

LAURA NUMEROFF'S children's book *If You Give a Moose a Muffin* shows how one simple act can lead to an uncontrollable situation: "If you give a moose a muffin, he'll want some jam to go with it. So you'll bring out some of your mother's homemade blackberry jam. When he's finished eating the muffin, he'll want another. And another. And another. When they're all gone, he'll ask you to make more. You'll have to go to the store to get some muffin mix. He'll want to go with you."[1] And so on.

Our desires can have a simple, innocent beginning but can also lead us down a path of uncontrolled passions and disastrous consequences. But we are not at the mercy of our desires. In ancient Greece (and in the culture of the New Testament era), self-control was a statement of power—not over others, but over oneself.[2] By identifying this as a fruit of the Spirit, Paul shows us that we humans cannot bear this power consistently and increasingly on our own: To master ourselves, we must lean ever more into the Holy Spirit and allow His work in us to keep us on the right path. In 1 Corinthians, Paul urges us to practice self-control.

---

1. Read 1 Corinthians 9:24–10:13. What illustrative examples does Paul use in these verses?

Paul's first example, of running a race (9:24-27), would have spoken to the Gentiles in the Corinthian church; the Isthmian athletic games were held in Corinth.[3] Paul's example of Moses and the Israelites in the wilderness (10:1-10) would have been aimed at the smaller Jewish population in the church.[4]

Galatians 5:23 and 1 Corinthians 9:27 (ESV, CSB) use different words to get at the same idea. Self-control (*enkrateia*) in Galatians 5 involves mastering one's "desires and passions"[5]; self-control or discipline (*hypōpiazō*) in 1 Corinthians 9 means to subdue one's passions.[6]

2. What key words and phrases in this passage help us understand the difference between self-control and lack of self-control?

New Testament scholar Craig Blomberg writes: "In verses 24-26a, Paul reminds the Corinthians that not all who run in a race receive the prize for first-place—a 'crown' (actually a pine wreath) that 'will not last' (literally, 'corruptible'). He does not want any of the members of his church to fail to get their spiritual and incorruptible crowns. Because this is an analogy, we must not press the correspondence too far. Paul scarcely imagines that there will be only one faithful Christian on Judgment Day!"[7]

3. Read 1 Corinthians 9:24-27. The city of Corinth hosted the Isthmian Games every other year, so the Corinthians would have known about athletic training and competition. What similarities and contrasts does Paul see between athletic competition and the Christian life (see verses 24-25)?

4. How do Paul's training and attitude provide a model of "self-control" (verse 25, ESV) or "self-discipline" (heading, NIV) for us today?

"Verse 27b has been taken as Paul's concern that he might lose his salvation (a remarkable thought in view of Rom. 8:31-38) or that 'the prize' refers to some kind of rewards above and beyond eternal life itself (an idea for which there is no shred of contextual support). More probably, 'disqualified' (*adokimos*) should be interpreted in light of the other reference to testing in the context of Judgment Day in 1 Corinthians (3:12-15). There Paul says God will 'test' (*dokimasei*; v. 13) believers' works and give out corresponding praise or censure. . . . But neither one's salvation nor eternal status in heaven is at stake."[8]

5. Read 1 Corinthians 10:1-13. What spiritual privileges did the Israelites have, and how do they parallel Christian experiences (see verses 1-5)?

6. Paul tells us that the Israelites are powerful negative examples for us today (see verse 6). In what specific ways did they disobey God, and what were the results in each case (see verses 6-10)?

7. What are some ways in which these same temptations plague Christians today?

8. How do the examples of Israel's sins provide stern warnings for us today (see verses 11-12)?

Craig Blomberg explains that "verse 11 repeats the warning of verse 6, all the more crucial since Christians live in the climactic era of human history for which all previous ages were preparing. Verse 12 summarizes the significance of these warnings for the Corinthians—even those who think they stand securely should take care, like Paul in 9:27, lest they fall and be disqualified."[9]

9. After such stern warnings, Paul encourages us in verse 13. How does it help you to know that any temptation you face is "common to mankind"?

"Verses 1-12 are all balanced by the marvelous promise of verse 13. The circumstances that tempt us to sin are never qualitatively different from those which God's people of every era have experienced, and we never have to give in to them. There is always an escape-hatch, which is defined as a way to persevere without sinning in whatever difficult situation we find ourselves."[10]

10. Some temptations seem unbearable. How does Paul assure us that God will help us in those situations (see verse 13)?

11. Self-control as part of the fruit of the Spirit means that the power we have over ourselves and our actions can help us be increasingly aligned with the will and conviction of the Holy Spirit. How does self-control influence our relationships in the body of Christ and our witness to a watching world?

Your Response

What have you learned in this passage about the vital importance of self-control or self-discipline in your life?

In what areas do you need to exhibit greater self-control?

For Further Study

How does David's experience with Bathsheba (2 Samuel 11) provide a real-life example of the ways even "a man after [God's] own heart" (Acts 13:22) can fall into temptation?

How does James 4:1-10 explain the consequences of ungodly desires and offer a way to avoid them?

NOTES

SESSION ONE—LOVE: LEARNING TO SERVE OTHERS

1. "'All You Need Is Love' History," accessed January 12, 2022, http://www.beatlesebooks.com/all-you-need-is-love.
2. Darrell L. Bock, *Luke: The NIV Application Commentary* (Grand Rapids, MI: Zondervan, 1996), 299.
3. R. T. France, *Luke: Teach the Text Commentary Series* (Grand Rapids, MI: Baker, 2013), 190.

SESSION TWO—JOY: REJOICING IN ANY SITUATION

1. Blue Letter Bible, "Lexicon: Strong's G5463—*chairō*," accessed January 12, 2022, https://www.blueletterbible.org/lexicon/g5463/kjv/tr/0-1/.
2. Tremper Longman III, ed., *The Baker Illustrated Bible Dictionary* (Grand Rapids, MI: Baker Books, 2013), s.v. "Praetorian Guard."
3. Frank Thielman, *Philippians: The NIV Application Commentary* (Grand Rapids, MI: Zondervan, 1995), 62.
4. Thielman, *Philippians*, 75.

SESSION THREE—PEACE: OVERCOMING ANXIETY

1. Frank Thielman, *Philippians: The NIV Application Commentary* (Grand Rapids, MI: Zondervan, 1995), 219.
2. Bible Hub, Strong's Hebrew Concordance on Bible Hub, "7965. *shalom*," accessed January 25, 2022, https://biblehub.com/hebrew/7965.htm.

SESSION FOUR—PATIENCE: THE BENEFITS OF WAITING

1. Thayer's Greek Lexicon entry in Blue Letter Bible, "Lexicon: Strong's G3114—*makrothymeō*," accessed January 13, 2022, https://www.blueletterbible.org/lexicon/g3114/kjv/tr/0-1/.
2. "'Therefore' in 5:7 (ESV, CSB) indicates that this section is the response of faith to the wickedness of the unjust landowner presented in the preceding section." Dan G. McCartney, *James: Baker Exegetical Commentary on the New Testament* (Grand Rapids, MI: Baker Academic, 2009), 240.

3. Blue Letter Bible, "Lexicon: Strong's G3114—*makrothymeō*."
4. Dan G. McCartney, *James: Baker Exegetical Commentary on the New Testament* (Grand Rapids, MI: Baker Academic, 2009), 242.
5. McCartney, *James*, 243.

SESSION FIVE—KINDNESS: CARING FOR ANOTHER

1. Elinor Evans, "5 Acts of Kindness That Changed History," HistoryExtra, February 17, 2020, https://www.historyextra.com/period/20th-century/acts-kindness-history-examples-jane-austen-harriet-tubman-elizabeth-fry-jesse-owens-berlin-olympics-miep-gies-anne-frank/.
2. Larry Schwartz, "Owens Pierced a Myth," ESPN.com, accessed January 13, 2022, https://www.espn.com/sportscentury/features/00016393.html.
3. K. Lawson Younger Jr., *Judges and Ruth: The NIV Application Commentary* (Grand Rapids, MI: Zondervan Academic, 2002), 440.
4. Younger, *Judges and Ruth*, 430.
5. Younger, *Judges and Ruth*, 439–40.
6. Younger, *Judges and Ruth*, 445.
7. Younger, *Judges and Ruth*, 446.

SESSION SIX—GOODNESS: OVERCOMING EVIL WITH GOOD

1. Emily Foreman, *We Died Before We Came Here: A True Story of Sacrifice and Hope* (Colorado Springs: NavPress, 2016), 145.
2. Blue Letter Bible, "Lexicon: Strong's G19—*agathōsynē*," accessed January 13, 2022, https://www.blueletterbible.org/lexicon/g19/kjv/tr/0-1/.
3. Douglas J. Moo, *Romans: The NIV Application Commentary* (Grand Rapids, MI: Zondervan, 2000), 412.
4. Moo, *Romans*, 412–13.
5. Moo, *Romans*, 413.

SESSION SEVEN—FAITHFULNESS: KEEPING OUR COMMITMENTS

1. Blue Letter Bible, "Lexicon: Strong's G4102—*pistis*," accessed January 13, 2022, https://www.blueletterbible.org/lexicon/g4102/kjv/tr/0-1/ and Blue Letter Bible, "Lexicon: Strong's G4103—*pistos*," accessed January 13, 2022, https://www.blueletterbible.org/lexicon/g4103/kjv/tr/0-1/.
2. D. A. Carson, "Matthew," in *The Expositor's Bible Commentary*, Volume 2, ed. Kenneth L. Barker and John R. Kohlenberger III (Grand Rapids, MI: Zondervan, 1994), 114.
3. Carson, "Matthew," 114.
4. Michael J. Wilkins, *Matthew: The NIV Application Commentary* (Grand Rapids, MI: Zondervan, 2004), 807.
5. Wilkins, *Matthew*, 808.

SESSION EIGHT—GENTLENESS: A PARENT'S CARE

1. Matt Mikalatos, *Journey to Love: What We Long for, How to Find It, and How to Pass It On* (Colorado Springs: NavPress, 2021), 29–30.

2. Blue Letter Bible, "Lexicon: Strong's G4240—*prautēs*," accessed January 13, 2022, https://www.blueletterbible.org/lexicon/g4240/kjv/tr/0-1/.
3. Michael W. Holmes, *1 & 2 Thessalonians: The NIV Application Commentary* (Grand Rapids, MI: Zondervan, 1998), 64n14.
4. Holmes, *1 & 2 Thessalonians*, 64–65.
5. Holmes, *1 & 2 Thessalonians*, 67.
6. Holmes, *1 & 2 Thessalonians*, 68.

SESSION NINE—SELF-CONTROL: MASTERING OUR DESIRES

1. Laura Numeroff, *If You Give a Moose a Muffin* (New York: HarperCollins, 1991).
2. Werner Jaeger, *Paideia: The Ideals of Greek Culture—Volume 2: In Search of the Divine Centre* (Oxford: Oxford University Press, 1943), 52–57.
3. *Britannica*, s.v. "Isthmian Games," accessed January 13, 2022, https://www.britannica.com/sports/Isthmian-Games.
4. "What Was the City and Church of Corinth Like?—An Excerpt from Ralph Martin's '2 Corinthians (WBC),'" Zondervan Academic, November 21, 2014, https://zondervanacademic.com/blog/what-was-the-city-and-church-of-corinth-like-an-excerpt-from-ralph-martins-2-corinthians-wbc.
5. Blue Letter Bible, "Lexicon: Strong's G1466—*egkrateia*," accessed January 13, 2022, https://www.blueletterbible.org/lexicon/g1466/niv/mgnt/0-1/.
6. Blue Letter Bible, "Lexicon: Strong's G5299—*hypōpiazō*," accessed January 13, 2022, https://www.blueletterbible.org/lexicon/g5299/kjv/tr/0-1/.
7. Craig L. Blomberg, *1 Corinthians: The NIV Application Commentary* (Grand Rapids, MI: Zondervan, 1994), 185.
8. Blomberg, *1 Corinthians*, 185.
9. Blomberg, *1 Corinthians*, 193.
10. Blomberg, *1 Corinthians*, 193.